Bright Baby Blankets

MW00913223

For colorful blankets that will delight Baby, choose from these fun crochet designs featuring Red Heart® yarns. Best-selling Super Saver® comes in more than 100 wonderful colors. Soft Baby Steps® is the ultimate yarn for babies in fresh, no-dye-lot solids and coordinating prints. Sweetest of all, Buttercup® has tiny pom-poms of color blended with a fleecy yarn that is squeezably soft.

About Red Heart® Yarns

Red Heart is one of the most trusted brands in yarn. For over 75 years more people have chosen to make American heirlooms using Red Heart yarn than any other yarn. Red Heart yarns stand for quality, largest color selection, fashion and above all else, crafted with love. Whatever your creativity calls for, you'll find it in the Red Heart family.

LEISURE ARTS, INC.
Maumelle, Arkansas

hexagon baby blanket

Designed by Ann Regis.

◖■◗ ◘◘ **EASY**

Blanket measures 43" wide x 48" deep (109 cm x 122 cm).

SHOPPING LIST

Yarn (Medium Weight)
RED HEART® Soft Baby Steps®:
- ☐ 9600 White **A** - 1 skein
- ☐ 9200 Baby Yellow **B** - 1 skein
- ☐ 9505 Aqua **C** - 4 skeins

Crochet Hook
- ☐ 6 mm [US J-10]

Additional Supplies
- ☐ Yarn needle
- ☐ Stitch markers

GAUGE INFORMATION
15 dc and 8 rows = 4" (10 cm).
Each motif measures 9" (23 cm) across. **CHECK YOUR GAUGE.**
Use any size hook to obtain the specified gauge.

hdc2tog (half double crochet 2 together): [Yo, insert hook into designated st or space, yo and pull up a loop] twice, yo and draw through all 5 loops on hook.

dc2tog (double crochet 2 together): [Yo, insert hook into designated st or space, yo and pull up a loop, yo and draw through 2 loops on hook] twice, yo and draw through all 3 loops on hook.

reverse sc: With right side facing, work sc from left to right *(Figs. 5a-d, page 44)*.

BLANKET
Motif A (Make 8)

With **A**, ch 6; join with a slip st to form a ring.

Round 1 (Right side): Ch 4 **(counts as tr, ch 1)**, [tr in ring, ch 1] 11 times; join with a slip st to 3rd ch of beginning ch-4 — 12 ch-1 spaces. Fasten off.

Round 2: With right side facing, join **B** with a slip st in any ch-1 space; ch 4 **(counts as tr, here and throughout)**, tr in same space, ch 1, *2 tr in next ch-1 space, ch 1; repeat from * around; join with a slip st to top of beginning ch-4 — 12 ch-1 spaces. Fasten off.

Round 3: With right side facing, join **C** with a slip st in any ch-1 space; ch 3 **(counts as dc, here and throughout)**, dc in same space, *dc between next 2 tr *(Fig. 3, page 42)*, 2 dc in next ch-1 space, dc between next 2 tr**, (2 dc, ch 2, 2 dc) in next ch-1 space; repeat from * around, ending last repeat at **, end with 2 dc in same ch-1 space as beginning ch-3, ch 1, sc in top of first ch-3 to form last ch-2 space — 8 dc across each side.

Round 4: Ch 3, dc in each dc across to next ch-2 space, *(dc, ch 2, dc) in next ch-2 space, dc in each of next 8 dc; repeat from * around, end with dc in first ch-2 space, ch 1, sc in top of beginning ch-3 to form last ch-2 space — 10 dc across each side.

Round 5: Ch 3, *dc in each dc across to next ch-2 space, (dc, ch 2, dc) in ch-2 space; repeat from * around, dc in each dc across to beginning, dc in first ch-2 space, ch 1, sc in top of beginning ch-3 to form last ch-2 space — 12 dc across each side.

Rounds 6 and 7: Repeat Round 5 twice — 16 dc across each side in Round 7. Fasten off.

Motif B (Make 6)

Work same as Motif A, using **B** for ring and Round 1, **A** for Round 2 and **C** for Rounds 3-7.

FINISHING

With **C**, whipstitch motifs together *(Fig. 4b, page 43)* following Assembly Diagram.

ASSEMBLY DIAGRAM

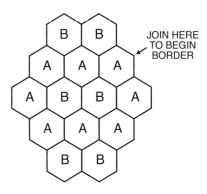

5

Border

With right side facing, join **C** with a slip st in ch-2 space as indicated on Assembly Diagram, page 5.

Round 1: Ch 3, dc in next 15 dc, dc2tog worked across next dc and next ch-2 space, place marker in last st, skip seam between motifs, dc2tog worked across next ch-2 space and next dc, [dc in next 15 dc, (dc, ch 2, dc) in next ch-2 space] twice, dc in next 15 dc, dc2tog worked across next dc and next ch-2 space, place marker in last st, skip seam between motifs, dc2tog worked across next ch-2 space and next dc, continue around, working dc in each dc, 2 decreases at each valley and (dc, ch 2, dc) in each ch-2 space around, ending with dc in same ch-2 space as beginning ch-3, ch 1, sc in top of beginning ch-3 to form last ch-2 space.

Note: In Rounds 2-7, continue to move markers up to first decrease at each valley.

Round 2: Ch 3, *dc in each dc across to 2 sts before marker, [dc2tog over next 2 sts] twice, [dc in each st across to next ch-2 space, (dc, ch 2, dc) in next ch-2 space] twice, continue working dc in each st around, working 2 decreases at each valley and (dc, ch 2, dc) in each ch-2 space, ending with dc in same ch-2 space as beginning ch-3, ch 1, sc in top of beginning ch-3 to form last ch-2 space. Fasten off.

Round 3: With right side facing, join **B** with a slip st in last ch-2 space; repeat Round 2.

Round 4: With right side facing, join **A** with a slip st in last ch-2 space; ch 2 (**counts as hdc**), *hdc in each dc across to 2 sts before marker, [hdc2tog over next 2 sts] twice, [hdc in each dc across to next ch-2 space, (hdc, ch 2, hdc) in ch-2 space] twice, continue working hdc in each st around, working 2 decreases at each valley and (hdc, ch 2, hdc) in each ch-2 space, ending with hdc in same ch-2 space as beginning ch-2, ch 1, sc in top of beginning ch-2 to form last ch-2 space. Fasten off.

Round 5: With **B**, repeat Round 3.

Round 6: With **C**, repeat Round 3 but do not fasten off.

Round 7: Ch 1, working from **left** to **right**, reverse sc in each st around working 1 reverse sc in each ch-2 space; join with a slip st to first reverse sc. Fasten off.

Weave in ends.

7

squares 'n squares baby blanket

Designed by Dee Phillips.

 **EASY**

Blanket measures 33½" x 33½" square (85 cm x 85 cm).

SHOPPING LIST

Yarn (Medium Weight)
RED HEART® Super Saver®:
☐ 995 Ocean - 4 skeins

Crochet Hook
☐ 4.5 mm [US G-7]

Additional Supplies
☐ Yarn needle

GAUGE INFORMATION
Each Square = 5¼" (13.25 cm).
CHECK YOUR GAUGE. Use any size hook to obtain the specified gauge.

BLANKET

Square (Make 36)

Ch 4; join with a slip st to form a ring.

Round 1 (Right side): Ch 3 **(counts as dc here and throughout)**, 15 dc in ring; join with a slip st to top of beginning ch-3 — 16 dc.

Round 2: Ch 3, 2 dc in same st as joining, ch 2, skip next dc, dc in next dc, ch 2, skip next dc, [3 dc in next dc, ch 2, skip next dc, dc in next dc, ch 2, skip next dc] 3 times; join with a slip st to top of beginning ch-3 — 8 ch-2 spaces.

Round 3: Ch 3, 5 dc in next dc, (dc in next dc, ch 2) twice, [dc in next dc, 5 dc in next dc, (dc in next dc, ch 2) twice] 3 times; join with a slip st to top of beginning ch-3 — 32 dc and 8 ch-2 spaces.

Round 4: Ch 3, dc in next 2 dc, 5 dc in next dc, dc in next 3 dc, ch 2, dc in next dc, ch 2, [dc in next 3 dc, 5 dc in next dc, dc in next 3 dc, ch 2, dc in next dc, ch 2] 3 times; join with a slip st to top of beginning ch-3 — 48 dc and 8 ch-2 sps.

Round 5: Ch 3, dc in next 4 dc, (2 dc, ch 1, 2 dc) in next dc (corner made), dc in next 5 dc, ch 2, dc in next dc, ch 2, [dc in next 5 dc, (2 dc, ch 1, 2 dc) in next dc (corner made), dc in next 5 dc, ch 2, dc in next dc, ch 2] 3 times; join with a slip st to top of beginning ch-3 — 60 dc and 12 spaces.
Fasten off.

FINISHING

Whipstitch Squares together through both loops *(Fig. 4a, page 43)*, 6 squares across and 6 squares down.

Border

Round 1: With right side facing, join yarn with a slip st in any corner ch-1 space; ch 5 (**counts as dc and ch 2**), [dc in same ch-1 space, ch 2] twice, *skip next 3 dc, dc in next dc, ch 2, skip next 2 dc, dc in next dc, [ch 2, dc in next dc] twice, ch 2, skip next 2 dc, dc in next dc, ch 2; repeat from * around working [dc, ch 2] 3 times in corner ch-1 spaces; join with a slip st to 3rd ch of beginning ch-5.

Round 2: Slip st in next ch-2 space, ch 3, 3 dc in same ch-2 space, slip st in next dc, [4 dc in next ch-2 space, slip st in next ch-2 space] twice, *[3 hdc in next dc, slip st in next ch-2 space, 4 dc in next ch-2 space] across to 3rd dc before first dc of next corner, 3 hdc in next dc, [slip st in next ch-2 space, 4 dc in next ch-2 space] twice, slip st in next dc, 4 dc in next ch-2 space, slip st in next ch-2 space, 4 dc in next ch-2 space; repeat from * around to last dc before last 3 ch-2 spaces on last side, 3 hdc in last dc, slip st in next ch-2 space, 4 dc in next ch-2 space, slip st in next ch-2 space; join with a slip st to top of beginning ch-3. Fasten off.

Weave in ends.

monkey around baby blanket

Designed by Michele Wilcox.

 **INTERMEDIATE**

Blanket measures 38" x 38" square (96.5 cm x 96.5 cm).

SHOPPING LIST

Yarn (Medium Weight) **4 MEDIUM**
RED HEART® Super Saver®:
- ☐ 316 Soft White **A** - 1 skein
- ☐ 319 Cherry Red **B** - 1 skein
- ☐ 336 Warm Brown **C** - 1 skein
- ☐ 672 Spring Green **D** - 1 skein
- ☐ 324 Bright Yellow **E** - 1 skein
- ☐ 385 Royal **F** - 1 skein
- ☐ 254 Pumpkin **G** - 1 skein
- ☐ 512 Turqua **H** - 1 skein
- ☐ 505 Aruba Sea **I** - 1 skein
- ☐ 312 Black **J** - 1 skein

Crochet Hook
- ☐ 5.5 mm [US I-9]

Additional Supplies
- ☐ Yarn needle

GAUGE INFORMATION
Each Square measures 7¼" (18.5 cm). **CHECK YOUR GAUGE.**
Use any size hook to obtain the specified gauge.

— SPECIAL STITCHES —

BPdc (Back Post double crochet):
Yo, insert hook from the back to front to back again around the post of designated st *(Fig. 2, page 42)*, yo and pull up a loop, [yo and draw through 2 loops on hook] twice.

FPdc (Front Post double crochet):
Yo, insert hook from the front to back to front again around the post of designated st *(Fig. 2, page 42)*, yo and pull up a loop, [yo and draw through 2 loops on hook] twice.

BLANKET
Solid Square
(Make 2 each with B, D, E, F, G and H; make 4 with I)
Ch 4; join with a slip st to form a ring.

Round 1 (Right side): Ch 3 **(counts as dc here and throughout)**, 11 dc in ring; join with a slip st to top of beginning ch-3 — 12 dc.

Round 2: Ch 3, FPdc around the post of same dc, *dc in next dc, FPdc around the post of same dc; repeat from * around; join with a slip st to top of beginning ch-3 — 24 sts.

Round 3: Ch 3, dc in next st, FPdc around the post of same FPdc, *dc in each of next 2 sts, FPdc around the post of same FPdc; repeat from * around; join with a slip st to top of beginning ch-3 — 36 sts.

Round 4: Ch 3, dc in next 2 sts, FPdc around the post of same FPdc, *dc in each of next 3 sts, FPdc around the post of same FPdc; repeat from * around; join with a slip st to top of beginning ch-3 — 48 sts.

Round 5: Ch 3, dc in next 3 sts, FPdc around the post of same FPdc, *dc in each of next 4 sts, FPdc around the post of same FPdc; repeat from * around; join with a slip st to top of beginning ch-3 — 60 sts.

Round 6: Ch 4 (**counts as tr**), working in back loops only *(Fig. 1, page 42)*, *dc in next st, hdc in next st, sc in each of next 9 sts, hdc in next st, dc in next st, tr in next st, ch 2**, tr in next st (corner made); repeat from * around, ending last repeat at **; join with a slip st to top of beginning ch-4 — 60 sts and 4 corner ch-2 spaces.

Round 7: Ch 1, sc in same st as joining and in each of next 14 sts, *5 sc in next ch-2 space (corner made)**, sc in each of next 15 sts; repeat from * around, ending last repeat at **; join with a slip st to first sc — 80 sc. Fasten off, leaving a long end for sewing.

Monkey Square
(Make 2 each using E, F, G and H for 2nd color; make 1 using D for 2nd color)
With **C**, work same as Solid Square through Round 5. Fasten off.

Rounds 6 and 7: With right side facing, join 2nd color with a slip st in same st as joining; repeat Rounds 6 and 7 of Solid Square.

Monkey Face (Make 9)

With **A**, ch 4.

Round 1 (Right side): 11 Dc in 4th ch from hook; join with a slip st to top of beginning ch-4 — 12 sts.

Round 2: Ch 3, dc in same st as joining, 2 dc in each dc around; join with a slip st to top of beginning ch-3 — 24 dc.

Round 3: Ch 1, 2 sc in same st as joining, sc in each of next 3 dc, *2 sc in next dc, sc in each of next 3 dc; repeat from * around; join with a slip st to first sc — 30 sc.

Round 4: Skip next 2 sc, 9 dc in next sc, skip next 2 sc, slip st in next 3 sc, skip next 2 sc, 9 dc in next sc, skip next 2 sc, slip st in next sc. Fasten off, leaving a long end for sewing.

EMBROIDERY

With **J**, embroider 2 satin stitch eyes *(Fig. 8, page 45)* and 2 French knot nostrils *(Fig. 7, page 45)*; with **B**, embroider backstitch smile as pictured *(Fig. 6, page 45)*. Sew 1 Monkey Face to center of each Monkey Square as pictured.

Ear (Make 18)

With **C**, ch 2.

Round 1 (Right side): 6 Sc in 2nd ch from hook; join with a slip st to first sc.

Round 2: Ch 3, dc in same st as joining, 2 dc in each st around; join with a slip st to top of beginning ch-3 — 12 dc.

Round 3: Ch 1, sc in same st as joining, 2 sc in next dc, *sc in next dc, 2 sc in next dc; repeat from * around; join with a slip st to first sc — 18 sc. Fasten off, leaving a long end for sewing. Sew in place on sides of each Monkey Face.

FINISHING

Whipstitch Squares together *(Fig. 4b, page 43)* following Assembly Diagrams.

ASSEMBLY DIAGRAMS

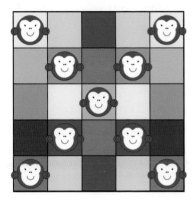

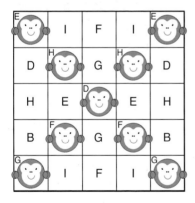

Border

Round 1: With right side facing, join **A** with a sc in first sc of any 5-sc corner *(see Joining With Sc, page 42)*; sc in same sc, 2 sc in each of next 4 sc (corner made), *sc in each st across to next 5-sc corner**, 2 sc in each of next 5 sc (corner made); repeat from * around, ending last repeat at **; join with a slip st to first sc.

Round 2: Ch 3, dc in each of next 3 sc, 3 dc in each of next 2 sc (corner made), *dc in each sc across to next 10-sc corner**, dc in each of next 4 sc, 3 dc in each of next 2 sc (corner made); repeat from * around, ending last repeat at **; join with a slip st to top of beginning ch-3.

Round 3: Ch 1, sc in same st as joining, *skip next dc, 6 dc in next dc, skip next dc**, sc in next dc; repeat from * around, ending last repeat at **; join with a slip st to first sc. Fasten off.

Weave in ends.

cuddly baby blanket

Designed by Nanette M. Seale.

 **EASY**

Blanket measures 36" x 36" square (91.5 cm x 91.5 cm).

SHOPPING LIST

Yarn (Bulky Weight) **🧶 5** BULKY

RED HEART® Buttercup®:

☐ 4278 Carnival **A** - 7 skeins

Yarn (Medium Weight) **🧶 4** MEDIUM

RED HEART® Soft Baby Steps®:

☐ 9505 Aqua **B** - 1 skein

☐ 9620 Baby Green **C** - 1 skein

Crochet Hook

☐ 8 mm [US L-11]

Additional Supplies

☐ Yarn needle

GAUGE INFORMATION

10 sc and 10 rows = 4" (10 cm); 5 sc rows
plus one puff row = 2¾" (7 cm); 8 puffs = 4" (10 cm).

CHECK YOUR GAUGE. Use any size hook to obtain the specified gauge.

— SPECIAL STITCH —

Puff: Yo, insert hook in designated st, yo and pull up a loop (3 loops on hook), [yo, insert hook in same st, yo and pull up a loop] 2 times, yo and draw through all 7 loops on hook.

BLANKET

With **A**, ch 4; join with a slip st to form a ring.

Round 1 (Right side): Ch 1, [2 sc in ring, ch 2] 4 times; join with a slip st to first sc — 8 sc and 4 ch-2 spaces.

Round 2: Ch 1, sc in same sc as joining and in next sc, (sc, ch 2, sc) in next ch-2 space (corner made), [sc in next 2 sc, (sc, ch 2, sc) in next ch-2 space (corner made)] 3 times; join with a slip st to first sc — 16 sc and 4 corner ch-2 spaces.

Round 3: Ch 1, sc in same sc as joining and in next 2 sc, (sc, ch 2, sc) in next corner ch-2 space, [sc in next 4 sc, (sc, ch 2, sc) in next corner ch-2 space] 3 times, sc in last sc; join with a slip st to first sc — 24 sc and 4 corner ch-2 spaces.

Round 4: Ch 1, sc in same sc as joining and in each sc across to next corner ch-2 space, (sc, ch 2, sc) in corner ch-2 space, [sc in each sc across to next corner ch-2 space, (sc, ch 2, sc) in corner ch-2 space] 3 times, sc in each sc to end of round; join with a slip st to first sc — 32 sc and 4 corner ch-2 spaces.

Round 5: Repeat Round 4 — 40 sc and 4 corner ch-2 spaces. Drop, but do not fasten off **A**.

Round 6: With right side facing, join **B** with a slip st in first st; ch 2, work Puff in same st, ch 1 (to close Puff), *[work Puff in next st, ch 1] across to next corner ch-2 space, work (Puff, ch 2, Puff) in corner ch-2 space, ch 1; repeat from * 3 times more, [work Puff in next st, ch 1] to end of round; join with a slip st to first Puff — 48 Puffs and 4 corner ch-2 spaces. Fasten off **B**.

Round 7: Draw up loop of **A** in last ch-1 space of previous round, ch 1, *sc in each ch-1 space across to next corner ch-2 space, (sc, ch 2, sc) in corner ch-2 space, sc in next Puff; repeat from * 3 times more, sc in each ch-1 space to end of round; join with a slip st to first sc — 56 sc and 4 corner ch-2 spaces.

Rounds 8-11: Repeat Round 4, 4 times — 88 sc and 4 corner ch-2 spaces at the end of Round 11. Drop, but do not fasten off **A**.

Round 12: With **C**, repeat Round 6 — 96 Puffs and 4 corner ch-2 spaces. Fasten off **C**.

Rounds 13-17: Repeat Rounds 7-11 — 136 sc and 4 corner ch-2 spaces at the end of Round 17.

Rounds 18-29: Repeat Rounds 6-17.

Rounds 30-36: Repeat Rounds 6-12; do not fasten off **C** at end of Round 36. Fasten off **A**.

Round 37: With **C**, ch 1, sc in each ch-1 space around, working 3 sc in each corner ch-2 space; join with a slip st to first sc. Fasten off **C**.

Weave in ends.

rickrack baby ripple blanket

◖■□□ EASY

Blanket measures 36" x 36" square (91.5 cm x 91.5 cm).

SHOPPING LIST

Yarn (Medium Weight)
RED HEART® Soft Baby Steps®:
☐ 9600 White **A** - 3 skeins
☐ 9505 Aqua **B** - 1 skein
☐ 9620 Baby Green **C** - 1 skein
☐ 9700 Baby Pink **D** - 1 skein
☐ 9590 Lavender **E** - 1 skein

Crochet Hook
☐ 5.5 mm [US I-9]

GAUGE INFORMATION
18 sts = 4" (10 cm) in pattern stitch. **CHECK YOUR GAUGE.**
Use any size hook to obtain the specified gauge.

BLANKET
With **A**, ch 157.

Row 1 (Right side)**:** Sc in 2nd ch from hook, skip next ch, *sc in next 4 chs, 3 sc in next ch, sc in next 4 chs **, skip next 2 chs; repeat from * across to last 2 chs, ending at **, skip next ch, sc in last ch — 156 sc.

NOTE: Entire Blanket is worked in back loops only throughout *(Fig. 1, page 42)*.

Row 2: Ch 1, turn; sc in first sc, skip next sc, *sc in next 4 sc, 3 sc in next sc, sc in next 4 sc **, skip next 2 sc; repeat from * across to last 2 sc, ending at **, skip next sc, sc in last sc. Fasten off.

Work the following stripe sequence for the next 24 rows: *2 Rows with **B**, 2 rows with **C**, 2 rows with **D**, 2 rows with **E**; repeat from * twice more.

Row 3: With right side facing, join designated color with sc in first sc *(see Joining With Sc, page 42)*; skip next sc, *sc in next 4 sc, 3 sc in next sc, sc in next 4 sc **, skip next 2 sc; repeat from * across to last 2 sc, ending at **, skip next sc, sc in last sc.

Row 4: Ch 1, turn; sc in first sc, skip next sc, *sc in next 4 sc, 3 sc in next sc, sc in next 4 sc **, skip next 2 sc; repeat from * across to last 2 sc, ending at **, skip next sc, sc in last sc. Fasten off.

Rows 5-26: Continuing in stripe sequence, repeat Rows 3 and 4, 11 times.

Row 27: With right side facing, join White with sc in first sc; skip next sc, *sc in next 4 sc, 3 sc in next 4 sc **, skip next 2 sc; repeat from * across to last 2 sc, ending at **, skip next sc, sc in last sc.

Rows 28-93: Ch 1, turn; sc in first sc, skip next sc, *sc in next 4 sc, 3 sc in next sc, sc in next 4 sc **, skip next 2 sc; repeat from * across to last 2 sc, ending at **, skip next sc, sc in last sc.

Row 94: Ch 1, turn; sc in first sc, skip next sc, *sc in next 4 sc, 3 sc in next sc, sc in next 4 sc **, skip next 2 sc; repeat from * across to last 2 sc, ending at **, skip next sc, sc in last sc. Fasten off.

Rows 95-118: Repeat Rows 3 and 4 in the following stripe sequence: *2 Rows with **E**, 2 rows with **D**, 2 rows with **C**, 2 rows with **B**; repeat from * twice more.

Rows 119 and 120: With White, repeat Rows 3 and 4.

Weave in ends.

broomstick lace baby blanket

■■□□ **EASY**

Blanket measures 28" x 39" (71 cm x 99 cm).

SHOPPING LIST

Yarn (Medium Weight)
RED HEART® Super Saver®:
- ☐ 942 Melonberry - 3 skeins

Crochet Hook
- ☐ 6 mm [US J-10]

Knitting Needle
- ☐ 25 mm [US size 50] - 1 needle

Additional Supplies
- ☐ Yarn needle

GAUGE INFORMATION

18 sc = 4" (10 cm); 8 rows = 5" (12.75 cm). **CHECK YOUR GAUGE.**
Use any size needle/hook to obtain the specified gauge.

Note: For video on this technique, see
www.redheart.com/learn/videos/broomstick-lace.

SPECIAL TECHNIQUE

How to Work Broomstick Lace

Make a practice swatch:

With crochet hook, ch 20.

Row 1 (Right side): Holding needle in left hand, place last loop
of last chain on needle. Working backward (left to right) into
foundation chain, *insert hook in next chain, yo, pull loop through
and place on needle; repeat from * across — 20 loops on needle.

Row 2: Insert hook in center of first 5 loops, holding loops together
as one, yo and pull yarn through loops, ch 1, 5 sc in same set of
5 loops, sliding loops off needle, *insert hook in next set of 5 loops
and work 5 sc; repeat from * across — 4 groups of 5 sc.

Row 3: Pull up last loop and place on needle. Working in back loops
only *(Fig. 1, page 42)*, pull up a loop in each sc across — 20 loops.
Repeat Rows 2 and 3 for lace pattern, ending with Row 2 of pattern.

BLANKET
With crochet hook, ch 125.

Row 1 (Right side): Following Row 1 of How to Work Broomstick Lace instructions on page 28, place 125 loops on needle.

Rows 2-61: Repeat Rows 2 and 3 of How to Work Broomstick Lace, 30 times — 25 groups of 5 sc each; 125 loops.

Row 62: Repeat Row 2. Do not fasten off.

Top Edging
With crochet hook, working from left to right, sc in last st made *(Figs. 5a-d, page 44)* (reverse sc made), *ch 1, reverse sc in next st to right; repeat from * across. Fasten off.

Bottom Edging
With right side facing, working across opposite side of foundation ch, join yarn with a slip st in left hand corner of opposite end; repeat Top Edging.

Weave in ends.

polar bear blanket & hat

Designed by Michele Wilcox.

◖▰▱▱ **EASY**

Blanket measures 35" x 35" square (89 cm x 89 cm).
Hat fits 3-6 months.

SHOPPING LIST

Yarn (Medium Weight) **🧶4**
RED HEART® Soft Baby Steps®:
- ☐ 9932 Puppy Print **A** - 5 skeins
- ☐ 9620 Baby Green **B** - 2 skeins
- ☐ 9600 White **C** - 1 skein

Thread (Super Fine Weight) **🧶1**
AUNT LYDIA'S® Fashion Crochet Thread, Size 3™:
- ☐ 12 Black - Small amount

Crochet Hook
- ☐ 4 mm [US G-6]

Additional Supplies
- ☐ Split lock stitch marker
- ☐ Yarn needle
- ☐ Small amount of stuffing

GAUGE INFORMATION

3 repeats = 3" (7.5 cm) across; 3 rows = 2¾" (7cm) in pattern.
CHECK YOUR GAUGE. Use any size hook to obtain the specified gauge.

— SPECIAL STITCHES —

inc (increase): 2 Sc in next sc.
dec (decrease): [Pull up a loop
in next st] twice, yo and draw
through all 3 loops on hook.

BLANKET
Square (Make 15 A and 1 B)
Ch 36.

Row 1: Dc in 4th ch from hook,
*skip next 3 chs, (sc, ch 3, 3 dc)
in next ch; repeat from * across
to last 4 chs, skip next 3 chs, sc in
last ch.

Rows 2-13: Ch 3, turn; dc in first
sc, *skip next 3 dc, (sc, ch 3, 3 dc)
in next ch-3 space; repeat from *
across to last st, sc in top of ch-3.

Row 14 (Right side): Ch 3, turn;
dc in first sc, ch 2, sc in next
ch-3 space, *ch 3, sc in next
ch-3 space; repeat from * across
to last 3 sts, ch 3, dc in next sc,
skip next dc, dc in top of ch-3.
Fasten off, leaving a long end for
sewing.

Sew squares together 4 across,
and 4 down, having the green
square second from the right in
the second row.

Bear Appliqué
HEAD
Work in continuous rounds
without joining. Mark beginning
of round. Move marker up each
round.

Round 1 (Right side): With C, ch 2,
6 sc in 2nd ch from hook.

Round 2: 2 Sc in each sc around
— 12 sc.

Round 3: [Sc in next sc, inc] 6
times — 18 sc.

Round 4: [Sc in next 2 sc, inc] 6
times — 24 sc.

Round 5: [Sc in next 3 sc, inc] 6
times — 30 sc.

Round 6: Sc in next 2 sc, inc, [sc
in next 4 sc, inc] 5 times, sc in next
2 sc — 36 sc.

Round 7: [Sc in next 5 sc, inc] 6 times — 42 sc.

Round 8: Sc in next 3 sc, inc, [sc in next 6 sc, inc] 5 times, sc in next 3 sc — 48 sc.

Round 9: [Sc in next 7 sc, inc] 6 times — 54 sc.

Round 10: Sc in next 4 sc, inc, [sc in next 8 sc, inc] 5 times, sc in next 4 sc — 60 sc.

Round 11: [Sc in next 9 sc, inc] 6 times — 66 sc. Fasten off, leaving a long end for sewing.

SNOUT
Round 1: With **C**, ch 2, 6 sc in 2nd ch from hook.

Round 2: 2 Sc in each sc around — 12 sc.

Round 3: Sc in each sc around.

Round 4: [Sc in next sc, inc] 6 times — 18 sc.

Round 5: Sc in each sc around.

Round 6: [Sc in next 2 sc, inc] 6 times — 24 sc.

Round 7: [Sc in next 3 sc, inc] 6 times — 30 sc.

Round 8: [Sc in next 4 sc, inc] 6 times — 36 sc.

Round 9: [Sc in next 5 sc, inc] 6 times — 42 sc. Fasten off, leaving a long end for sewing.

Sew Snout in place on Head, stuffing lightly.
With crochet thread, embroider satin stitch eyes and nose *(Fig. 8, page 45)* and straight stitch mouth *(Fig. 9, page 45)*. Sew in place on **B** square.

EAR (Make 2)

Rounds 1-3: Work same as Head Rounds 1-3 — 18 sc.

Rounds 4-6: Sc in each sc around.

Round 7: [Sc in next sc, dec] 6 times — 12 sc. Fasten off. Do not stuff. Sew in place.

Blanket Edging

(Worked along each side separately)

Row 1: With right side facing, join **B** with a slip st in any corner; ch 1, work 120 sc evenly spaced across (30 sc across each square).

Row 2: Ch 1, turn; sc in each sc across.

Row 3: Ch 3, turn; skip first sc, dc in next sc and in each sc across.

Row 4: Ch 1, turn; sc in each dc across and in top of ch-3. Fasten off **B**.

Row 5: With right side facing, join **C** with a slip st in first sc; ch 1, sc in first 4 sc, *(slip st, ch 1, 9 hdc) in next sc, drop loop from hook, insert hook from front in first hdc, then into dropped loop, pull loop through, ch 1 to close, sc in next 9 sc; repeat from * across ending sc in last 5 sc. Fasten off.

Repeat Edging Rows 1-5 along each side.

Snowflake (Make 4)

With **C**, ch 6; join with a slip st to form a ring.

Round 1: Ch 1, 12 sc in ring; join with a slip st to first sc.

Round 2: Ch 3, 2 dc in same st as joining, ch 1, skip next sc, *3 dc in next sc, ch 1, skip next sc; repeat from * around; join with a slip st to top of beginning ch-3.

Round 3: Ch 1, sc in same st as joining, *(hdc, dc, ch 2, dc, hdc) in next dc, sc in next dc and in next ch-1 space **, sc in next dc; repeat from * around, ending at **; join with a slip st to first sc. Fasten off.

Sew one snowflake at each corner.

Weave in ends.

HAT

With **B**, ch 7.
Work in ribbing as follows:

Row 1: Sc in 2nd ch from hook and in each ch across — 6 sc.

Rows 2-65: Ch 1, turn; working in back loops only *(Fig. 1, page 42)*, sc in each sc across.

Crown

Row 1 (Right side)**:** Ch 1, sc in end of each row across ribbing — 65 sc. Fasten off **B**.

Row 2: With wrong side facing, join **A** with a slip st in first sc; ch 3, dc in same st as joining, *skip next 3 sc, (sc, ch 3, 3 dc) in next sc; repeat from * across to last 4 sc, skip next 3 sc, sc in last sc.

Rows 3-6: Ch 3, turn; dc in first sc, *skip next 3 dc, (sc, ch 3, 3 dc) in next ch-3 space; repeat from * across to last st, sc in top of ch-3.

Row 7: Ch 3, turn; dc in first sc, ch 2, sc in next ch-3 space, *ch 3, sc in next ch-3 space; repeat from * across to last 3 sts, ch 3, dc in next sc, skip next dc, dc in top of ch-3.

Row 8: Ch 1, turn; sc in first dc, skip next dc, sc in each sc and in each ch across, skip next dc, sc in top of ch-3 — 64 sc. Fasten off **A**.

Row 9: With right side facing, join **B** with a slip st in first sc; ch 1, sc in same sc and in next 13 sc, dec, [sc in next 14 sc, dec] 3 times — 60 sc.

Row 10: Ch 1, turn; [sc in next 8 sc, dec] 6 times — 54 sc.

Row 11: Ch 1, turn; [sc in next 7 sc, dec] 6 times — 48 sc.

Row 12: Ch 1, turn; [sc in next 6 sc, dec] 6 times — 42 sc.

Row 13: Ch 1, turn; [sc in next 5 sc, dec] 6 times — 36 sc.

Row 14: Ch 1, turn; [sc in next 4 sc, dec] 6 times — 30 sc.

Row 15: Ch 1, turn; [sc in next 3 sc, dec] 6 times — 24 sc.

Row 16: Ch 1, turn; [sc in next 2 sc, dec] 6 times — 18 sc.

Row 17: Ch 1, turn; [sc in next sc, dec] 6 times — 12 sc.

Row 18: Ch 1, turn; [dec] 6 times — 6 sc. Fasten off, leaving a long end for sewing. Sew back seam.

Polar Bear Earflaps
HEAD (Make 2)
Work in continuous rounds without joining. Mark beginning of round. Move marker up each round.

Round 1 (Right side): With **C**, ch 2, 6 sc in 2nd ch from hook.

Round 2: 2 Sc in each sc around — 12 sc.

Round 3: [Sc in next sc, inc] 6 times — 18 sc.

Round 4: [Sc in next 2 sc, inc] 6 times — 24 sc.

Round 5: [Sc in next 3 sc, inc] 6 times — 30 sc.

Round 6: Sc in next 2 sc, inc, [sc in next 4 sc, inc] 5 times, sc in next 2 sc — 36 sc.

Round 7: [Sc in next 5 sc, inc] 6 times — 42 sc.

Round 8: Slip st in each sc around. Fasten off.

EAR (Make 4)
Row 1: With **C**, ch 2, 4 sc in 2nd ch from hook.

Row 2: Ch 1, turn; 2 sc in each sc across — 8 sc.

Row 3: Ch 1, turn; sc in first 2 sc, [inc] 4 times, sc in last 2 sc — 12 sc. Fasten off, leaving a long end for sewing.

SNOUT (Make 2)
Round 1: With **C**, ch 2, 6 sc in 2nd ch from hook.

Round 2: 2 Sc in each sc around — 12 sc.

Round 3: Sc in each sc around.

Round 4: [Sc in next sc, inc] 6 times — 18 sc. Fasten off, leaving a long end for sewing.

Finishing
Sew 2 Ears in place on each Head. Sew Snouts in place. Embroider same as Bear on Blanket. Sew in place on each side of Hat.

Weave in ends.

coziest baby blanket ever

Designed by Michele Wilcox.

■□□□ **BEGINNER**

Blanket measures 30" x 32" (76 cm x 81.5 cm).

SHOPPING LIST

Yarn (Bulky Weight)
RED HEART® Buttercup®:
- ☐ 4273 Light Yellow Multi - 8 skeins

Crochet Hook
- ☐ 8 mm [US L-11]

Additional Supplies
- ☐ Yarn needle

GAUGE INFORMATION

8 double crochet and 5 rows = 4" (10 cm). **CHECK YOUR GAUGE.**
Use any size hook to obtain the specified gauge.

BLANKET

Chain 61.

Row 1: Double crochet in 2nd chain from hook and in each chain across — 60 double crochets.

Rows 2-41: Chain 2 (**counts as double crochet**), turn; working in front loops only (*Fig. 1, page 47*), double crochet in each double crochet across.

Fasten off.

Weave in ends.

general instructions

ABBREVIATIONS

A, B, etc.	color A, B, etc.
BPdc	Back Post double crochet(s)
ch(s)	chain(s)
cm	centimeters
dc	double crochet(s)
dc2tog	double crochet 2 together
dec	decrease
FPdc	Front Post double crochet(s)
hdc	half double crochet
hdc2tog	half double crochet 2 together
inc	increase
mm	millimeters
sc	single crochet(s)
st(s)	stitch(es)
tr	treble crochet(s)
yo	yarn over

SYMBOLS & TERMS

( ) **or** [ ] = work directions in parentheses or brackets the number of times specified.

* **or** ** = repeat whatever follows the * or ** as indicated.

CROCHET TERMINOLOGY	
UNITED STATES	INTERNATIONAL
slip stitch (slip st) =	single crochet (sc)
single crochet (sc) =	double crochet (dc)
half double crochet (hdc) =	half treble crochet (htr)
double crochet (dc) =	treble crochet (tr)
treble crochet (tr) =	double treble crochet (dtr)
double treble crochet (dtr) =	triple treble crochet (ttr)
triple treble crochet (tr tr) =	quadruple treble crochet (qtr)
skip =	miss

CROCHET HOOKS																
U.S.	B-1	C-2	D-3	E-4	F-5	G-6	7	H-8	I-9	J-10	K-10½	L-11	M/N-13	N/P-15	P/Q	Q	S
Metric - mm	2.25	2.75	3.25	3.5	3.75	4	4.5	5	5.5	6	6.5	8	9	10	15	16	19

GAUGE

Gauge refers to the number of stitches and rows in a given area. When making projects, ensure that your project is the correct finished size and is to gauge. Work the area as stated in the pattern and then measure to check that it agrees with the gauge given. If it is not the same size, change your hook size. If it is too large, use a smaller hook. If it is too small, use a larger hook size.

Yarn Weight Symbol & Names	LACE (0)	SUPER FINE (1)	FINE (2)	LIGHT (3)	MEDIUM (4)	BULKY (5)	SUPER BULKY (6)
Type of Yarns in Category	Fingering, 10-count crochet thread	Sock, Fingering Baby	Sport, Baby	DK, Light Worsted	Worsted, Afghan, Aran	Chunky, Craft, Rug	Bulky, Roving
Crochet Gauge* Ranges in Single Crochet to 4" (10 cm)	32-42 double crochets**	21-32 sts	16-20 sts	12-17 sts	11-14 sts	8-11 sts	5-9 sts
Advised Hook Size Range	Steel*** 6,7,8 Regular hook B-1	B-1 to E-4	E-4 to 7	7 to I-9	I-9 to K-10½	K-10½ to M/N-13	M/N-13 and larger

*GUIDELINES ONLY: The chart above reflects the most commonly used gauges and hook sizes for specific yarn categories.

** Lace weight yarns are usually crocheted on larger-size hooks to create lacy openwork patterns. Accordingly, a gauge range is difficult to determine. Always follow the gauge stated in your pattern.

*** Steel crochet hooks are sized differently from regular hooks–the higher the number the smaller the hook, which is the reverse of regular hook sizing.

■□□□ BEGINNER	Projects for first-time crocheters using basic stitches. Minimal shaping.
■■□□ EASY	Projects using yarn with basic stitches, repetitive stitch patterns, simple color changes, and simple shaping and finishing.
■■■□ INTERMEDIATE	Projects using a variety of techniques, such as basic lace patterns or color patterns, mid-level shaping and finishing.
■■■■ EXPERIENCED	Projects with intricate stitch patterns, techniques and dimension, such as non-repeating patterns, multi-color techniques, fine threads, small hooks, detailed shaping and refined finishing.

JOINING WITH SC

When instructed to join with sc, begin with a slip knot on hook. Insert hook in stitch or space indicated, yo and pull up a loop, yo and draw through both loops on hook.

BACK OR FRONT LOOP ONLY

Work only in loop(s) indicated by arrow *(Fig. 1)*.

Fig. 1

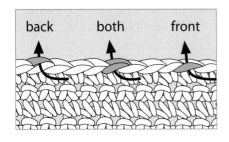

POST STITCH

Work around the post of the stitch indicated, inserting the hook in direction of the arrow *(Fig. 2)*.

Fig. 2

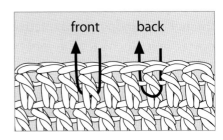

WORKING IN A SPACE BETWEEN STITCHES

When instructed to work in a space between stitches, insert hook into space indicated by arrow *(Fig. 3)*.

Fig. 3

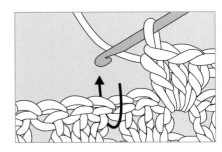

WHIPSTITCH

Place two Motifs or Squares with **wrong** sides together. Beginning in center st of corner, sew through both pieces once to secure the beginning of the seam, leaving an ample yarn end to weave in later. Insert the needle from **front** to **back** through **both** loops on **both** pieces *(Fig. 4a)* **or** through **inside** loops only of each stitch on **both** pieces *(Fig. 4b)*. Bring the needle around and insert it from **front** to **back** through next loops of both pieces. Continue in this manner across to corner, keeping the sewing yarn fairly loose.

Fig. 4a

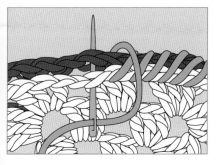

Fig. 4b

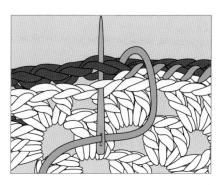

REVERSE SINGLE CROCHET

Working from **left** to **right**, *insert hook in st to right of hook *(Fig. 5a)*, yo and draw through, under and to the left of loop on hook (2 loops on hook) *(Fig. 5b)*, yo and draw through both loops on hook *(Fig. 5c)* *(reverse sc made, Fig. 5d)*; repeat from * around.

Fig. 5a

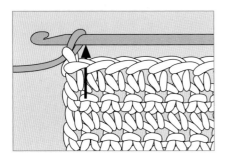

Fig. 5b

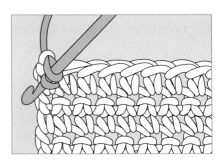

Fig. 5c

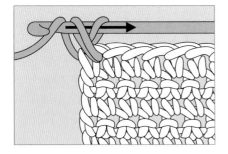

Fig. 5d

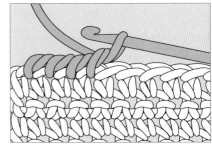

EMBROIDERY STITCHES

Backstitch

The backstitch is worked from right to left. Come up at 1, go down at 2 and come up at 3 *(Fig. 6)*. The second stitch is made by going down at 1 and coming up at 4.

Fig. 6

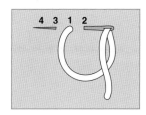

French Knot

Bring needle up at 1. Wrap yarn around the needle the desired number of times and insert needle at 2, holding end of yarn with non-stitching fingers *(Fig. 7)*. Tighten knot; then pull needle through, holding yarn until it must be released.

Fig. 7

Satin Stitch

Satin stitch is a series of straight stitches worked side-by-side so they touch but do not overlap. Come up at odd numbers and go down at even numbers *(Fig. 8)*.

Fig. 8

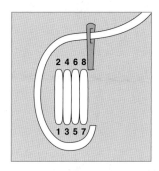

Straight Stitch

Straight stitch is just what the name implies, a single, straight stitch. Come up at 1 and go down at 2 *(Fig. 9)*.

Fig. 9

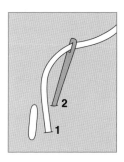

yarn information

The projects in this book were created with **RED HEART®** yarns. For best results, we recommend following the pattern exactly as written. Be sure to purchase the amounts recommended in the pattern, and retain your labels. Always follow the care instructions provided on the label.

RED HEART® Soft Baby Steps®
Art. E746 available in solid colors
5 oz (141 g), 256 yd (234 m), prints 4 oz (113 g), 204 yds (187 m) skeins

RED HEART® Super Saver®
Art. E300 available in solid colors
7 oz (198 g), 364 yd (333 m); multi colors, flecks and prints 5 oz (141 g), 244 yds (223 m) skeins

RED HEART® Buttercup®

Art. N396 available in 1.76 oz (50 g), 63 yd (57 m) skeins

AUNT LYDIA'S® Fashion Crochet Thread, Size 3™

Art. 182 available in solid colors 150 yds (137 m)
and metallic 100 yds (92 m) balls

For more ideas and inspiration
www.redheart.com
www.facebook.com/redheartyarns
www.pinterest.com/redheartyarns
www.twitter.com/redheartyarns
www.youtube.com/redheartyarns
Instagram@redheartyarns

We have made every effort to ensure that these instructions are accurate and complete. We cannot, however, be responsible for human error, typographical mistakes, or variations in individual work.

Copyright © 2015 by Leisure Arts, Inc., 104 Champs Blvd, STE 100, Maumelle, AR 72113-6738, www.leisurearts.com. All rights reserved. This publication is protected under federal copyright laws. Reproduction or distribution of this publication or any other Leisure Arts publication, including publications which are out of print, is prohibited unless specifically authorized. This includes, but is not limited to, any form of reproduction or distribution on or through the Internet, including posting, scanning, or e-mail transmission.

© 2015 Coats & Clark, all rights reserved.